SINGAPORE

Bruce Elder

General Editor
Henry Pluckrose

Franklin Watts
London   New York   Sydney   Toronto

Facts about Singapore

Area:
618 sq. km
(239 sq. miles)

Population:
2,472,000 (1982 estimate)

Capital:
Singapore

Official languages:
Chinese, Malay, Tamil,
English

Main religions:
Buddhism, Taoism,
Islam, Christianity,
Hinduism

Main exports:
Petroleum, machinery,
rubber, food

Currency:
Dollar

Franklin Watts Limited
12a Golden Square
London W1

Franklin Watts Inc.
387 Park Avenue South
New York N.Y. 10016

ISBN: UK Edition 0 86313 090 9
ISBN: US Edition 0-531-04942-6
Library of Congress Catalog Card No:
84-51808

© Franklin Watts Limited 1985

Text Editor: Brenda Williams
Maps: Tony Payne
Stamps: Stanley Gibbons Limited
Photographs: Singapore Tourist
Promotion Board; Bruce Elder, 25; Zefa,
6; J. Allan Cash, 7; Colorpix/Ron Carter,
19; John Topham Picture Library, 12;
Blue Circle Industries, 13
Front Cover: Colorpix/Ron Carter
Back Cover: Singapore Tourist
Promotion Board

Typeset by Ace Filmsetting Ltd,
Frome, Somerset
Printed in Hong Kong

Singapore is a small country at the
southern tip of the Malay peninsula
in South-east Asia. It includes one
large island, also called Singapore,
and about 50 small ones. A causeway
links Singapore island to the Malay
peninsula, which is part of Malaysia.

10918

The city of Singapore is the country's capital and is mostly modern. Areas of poor housing were replaced in the 1960s with new apartment blocks. Six new towns have been built and others planned.

About 77 out of every 100 people in Singapore are of Chinese origin, 15 have Malay ancestry, 6 are of Indian origin and 2 have other backgrounds.

Sir Stamford Raffles was allowed
to found a British port on Singapore
island in 1819. By 1824, the entire
island had become British. Raffles's
statue now stands where he landed.

Singapore became independent in 1963 as one of the 14 states in the Federation of Malaysia. But Singapore broke away and became a separate country in 1965. Its official name is now the Republic of Singapore. This is the Supreme Court.

This picture shows some stamps and money used in Singapore. The main unit of currency is the dollar, which is divided into 100 cents.

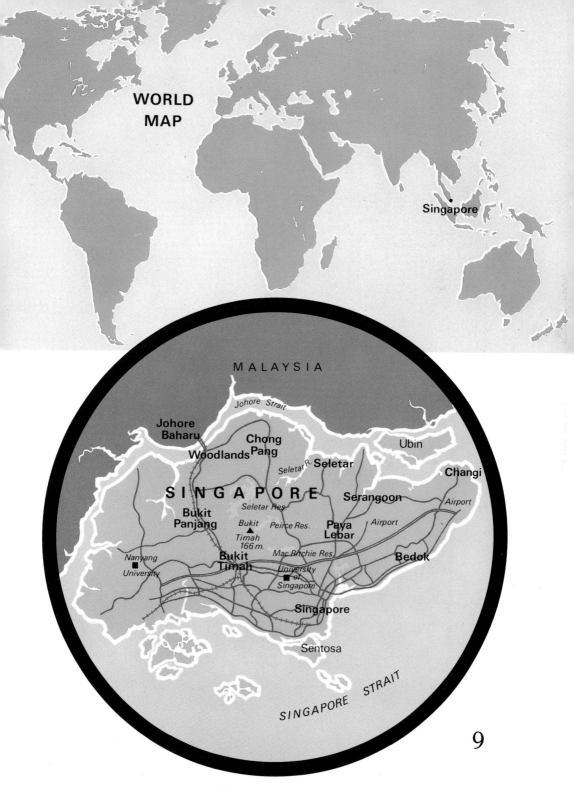

WORLD
MAP

Singapore

MALAYSIA

Johore Strait

Johore
Baharu

Chong
Pang

Woodlands

Ubin

Seletar R. Seletar

Changi

SINGAPORE

Serangoon

Airport

Seletar Res.

Bukit
Panjang

*Bukit
Timah
166 m.*

Peirce Res.

Paya
Lebar

Airport

Mac Ritchie Res.

Nanyang
University

Bukit
Timah

*University
of
Singapore*

Bedok

Singapore

Sentosa

SINGAPORE STRAIT

9

In the 19th century the port at Singapore grew quickly, partly because it was near the rubber plantations of the Malay peninsula. Rubber is still important for trade. Here, workers lift bales of rubber on to a barge.

Singapore is one of the world's busiest ports and trade is still an important source of money. Singapore's trade is mostly with Japan, Malaysia, the USA, Saudi Arabia and Europe.

Singapore is an important industrial country. More than 30 out of every 100 people work in industry, but only 1 in every 100 in farming and fishing. Jurong is Singapore's largest industrial estate.

Ships, steel products, chemicals, petroleum products, wood, plastics and textiles are leading industrial products, but most raw materials come from abroad. Limestone from this quarry is used to make cement.

Land is scarce in Singapore and food must be imported. But market gardeners can grow fruit and vegetables even in the shadow of apartment blocks. Pig and chicken farming are also important.

Singapore is famous for its markets. Some sell fresh fruits such as paw-paws and water-melons, which are ready to eat. Such fruits grow well in the hot, humid climate.

Chinese foods enjoyed in Singapore include "1,000-year-old eggs." These eggs are not really 1,000 years old. Instead, fresh eggs are left in clay for six to ten weeks before they are eaten. The eggs are green, rich and creamy. They have a fishy taste.

Restaurants of many kinds are found in Singapore. Chinese restaurants serve dishes from all the main regions of China. Indian, Indonesian and European restaurants are also popular.

Some people still live in old villages outside the modern town areas.
These villages are called kampongs.
Houses in the kampongs are made of wood and bamboo.

Some rich people in Singapore live in expensive houses, but most people live in apartment blocks. People dry their washing on poles which hang out from their balconies.

Children in Singapore must stay at school from the age of 6 to 16. The people believe that education is most important. Many want to become students at one of the country's 80 technical colleges or universities.

Customs and religions differ between the various groups of people in Singapore. Many people of Malay origin are Muslims, while most Indians are Hindus. This picture was taken at a Malay wedding.

Most people of Chinese ancestry in Singapore are Buddhists and Taoists. These families are celebrating a Taoist festival in a temple. They say prayers, light perfumed joss sticks and make offerings to the gods.

A calligrapher works in the Chinese
market area. Calligraphy is the art of
handwriting. The Chinese admire
this skill. Messages are written on
scrolls and wall hangings with a
brush.

2794

Trishaws are still used for journeys in the Chinese market area. These three-wheeled vehicles have a cab in which two people can sit. But this slow form of travel is used only for short trips.

Haw Par Villa is often called the Tiger Balm Gardens and is a popular place for visitors. It is a fantasy land, full of brightly painted statues. Each animal or person is a well known figure from Chinese stories.

Judo is a popular sport in Singapore, as are karate, boxing and jujitsu. These martial arts are enjoyed in many Asian countries.

People who live in the city's high apartment blocks must not keep cats or dogs. Instead, they have fishes and birds. At weekends, some owners take their birds to bird-singing contests.

The different peoples of Singapore hold their own festivals. The Hindu festival of Thaipusan is a day of penitence. The man in this picture has skewers stuck into his skin but feels no pain.

The Chinese celebrate their New Year in late January or early February. The following weekend, they hold the Chingay procession. Stilt walkers, decorated floats and dragon dancers are some of the attractions.

A growing number of tourists visit Singapore every year. Many go there to shop. Others enjoy its beaches and resorts. The small island of Sentosa, just south of the island of Singapore, is especially popular.

Since 1963, Singapore's manufacturing and other industries have grown enormously. Money earned from industry and trading has made Singapore wealthy. Its people now enjoy a higher standard of living than in many parts of Asia.

Index